¿Quién Es Mi Vecino?
Spanish as a Second Language,
Northern Illinois Conference of the United Methodist Church

¿Quién es mi vecino?
Who Is My Neighbor?

Learning Spanish as Church Hospitality:
A Worship-Centered Curriculum

Teacher's Manual

Joyce Carrasco, MTS
Ruth Cassel Hoffman, PhD
Ngoc-Diep Nguyen, PhD

¿QUIÉN ES MI VECINO?
WHO IS MY NEIGHBOR?
TEACHER'S MANUAL

ISBN 978-1-5018-0367-3

15 16 17 18 19 20 21 22 23 24–10 9 8 7 6 5 4 3 2 1
MANUFACTURED IN THE UNITED STATES OF AMERICA

Content

Foreword

"What are you doing this evening?" the woman who cuts my hair asked me.
"I'm going to a Spanish-as-Second-Language class."
"What's that?" she asked.

I explained to her that I wanted the people in the churches that I serve to learn to speak Spanish so that they can be more hospitable toward their neighbors. Not only in Illinois but throughout the United States, there is a large and/or growing population of Spanish-speaking people. While most of these new immigrants are eager to learn English and attend English classes, it's hospitable to at least attempt Spanish when we connect with them in our communities and in our churches.

"Wow! I never heard of anything like that! That's cool!" she said. Then she added, "I'd like to do that." I assured her that it wasn't exclusively for United Methodists but anyone who was interested.

This represents a typical conversation when talking about the Spanish-as-Second-Language classes being held in the Northern Illinois Annual Conference. After coming to Northern Illinois, I called together a small group of United Methodist linguists with my vision of a curriculum. I imagined it to be an adult learning experience that would enable us to speak if only minimally, sing with greater confidence, and pray together in our culturally diverse communities, churches and annual conference. These dedicated United Methodist linguists developed this curriculum that can assist us in being buenos vecinos (good neighbors).

The orientation for teachers and host church representatives is very important so that those who teach understand the spirit of the curriculum. It's also important that the host churches provide hospitality to those who come; many times people would come from other churches and from the community at large.

5

I went to the first orientation for the teachers and host church representatives after I signed up for my own six-week course but I was anxious about being able to learn any Spanish. I have a "foreign language anxiety." I learned at the orientation for the teachers and hosts that we would learn Spanish the way a child learns a language; not by conjugating verbs or memorizing long lists of words. We learned our first language by listening to it, seeking to comprehend it even when we didn't totally understand every word, and then slowly beginning to speak it…very slowly. Speaking is the hardest part and usually language courses quickly "force" adults into speaking before they're really comfortable doing it.

My foreign language anxiety was heightened again as I went to my first class but it was quickly reduced as the teacher guided us through the lesson plan. This curriculum is a model of adult learning with many participatory activities which resulted in lots of fun and laughter.

After attending several classes, I was privileged to attend the installation of the presiding bishop of the Evangelical Lutheran Church on the campus of the University of Chicago. And wouldn't you know? The person sitting next to me was the only Lutheran woman bishop in Latin America. There were no other Spanish-speaking persons around her. She spoke very little English and I spoke very, very little Spanish but she was patient and kind with me and I know she appreciated that I even tried. These experiences happen all the time in our daily lives, in the life of our church, and in our communities. It will happen to you and when it does, you'll be able to demonstrate hospitality through a few kind words!

This curriculum has been a labor of love by the women who have developed, tested and revised it over the last two years and I highly recommend it even (or maybe especially) if you have foreign language anxiety. In the classes I took, there were people with various levels of ability to speak Spanish already and this added to the class immensely. Whether you know no Spanish whatsoever or you took Spanish in high school (and it's been years since you used it), you'll benefit from this curriculum.

All of us live in communities where our neighbors are Spanish-speakers. It says a lot about the openness of our hearts, minds and doors when we speak a word to them, even if it is halting and without the right verb conjugation…

Bishop Sally Dyck

Starting Your Program

Directions and Forms for the Hosting Church

Host Site Commitment

¿Quién es mi vecino?

The NIC Spanish as a Second Language Task Force commits to the host church:

- We will provide and train a Spanish instructor for the class.

- We will provide the teaching materials, handouts for the students, and supplies.

- We will provide the curriculum. All classes in the NIC will be taught using the same curriculum, based on radical hospitality and meeting and welcoming our Spanish-speaking neighbors. We will, however, revise the curriculum as required to ensure that we are meeting the goals and objectives set out in our planning meetings.

- We will handle student registration for the classes.

- We will support the host sites by name in our prayers.

The host church commits to the NIC Spanish as a Second Language Task Force:

- We will provide an SSL Local Church Ambassador to oversee the logistics of holding this class on this site. The responsibilities of the SSL Local Church Ambassador are detailed on the attached sheet "SSL Local Church Ambassador Checklist". That Local Church Ambassador will attend the orientation for the class.

- All funds collected as registration fees or freewill offerings for these classes will be forwarded to the designated address at the NIC, for use in expanding this program to all districts of the NIC and to as many churches and individuals as possible.

- We will treat these classes as a ministry of our local congregation, and accord them the same importance as we give to other ministries.

- A standing committee of this congregation will adopt this ministry as its own.

- We will welcome the class attendees and make them feel at home.

- We will provide in-kind donations in the form of a rent-free meeting room, light, heat or air conditioning as needed, beverages and light snacks for class participants, and the use of a whiteboard, blackboard, or easel/paper for the classroom.

- We will support the classes and their participants with prayer.

Signatures:

_____

on behalf of host church   date

_____

host church - town: district

_____

on behalf of the SSL Task Force   date

Job Description: Spanish Teacher

Northern Illinois Conference of the United Methodist Church
"Who Is My Neighbor?" Spanish as a Second Language Classes

<u>Please read this document carefully before filling out the Job Application! It contains important information about this Spanish teaching program.</u>

Our mission

Spanish as a Second Language seeks to act upon the question answered by Jesus in His story of the Good Samaritan: Who is my neighbor? More importantly, it seeks to translate this seminal question into concrete action in our communities. It acknowledges the fact that in many cases Hispanic and Anglo communities do not mix, and that because of this we fail to fully serve God and love our neighbor.

The project seeks to break down the language and cultural barriers among us so that we can know our neighbors and understand their ways. We propose to accomplish this by giving our Anglo congregants the opportunity to learn the language of their neighbor, to enable them to speak--if only a little--with Hispanic neighbors. In so doing, the participants will themselves be transformed, and we will thus transform our relationships with those around us.

By focusing Spanish classes on ways in which we serve and love our neighbor, rather than on the usual grammatical or secular-activity approaches such as travel, we will open the doors for worshipping together (participants will be invited to worship in a Hispanic church) as well as eating together (the last class of the series includes a potluck), sharing each other's burdens, praying with and for each other, and truly becoming one in the Lord. We will be recreating the miracle of Pentecost.

The details

Each class will consist of six two-hour sessions taught over the course of six weeks. Other formats are possible, but each series will include twelve hours of instruction. The classes will meet in churches across Northern Illinois, throughout the six Districts of the Northern Illinois Conference: Aurora, Chicago Northwestern, Chicago Southern, DeKalb, Elgin, and Rockford. We will, of course, assign selected teachers to classes as near to them as possible.

We consider this course a ministry and a labor of love. We understand that teaching it is a sacrifice of your time. However, we are prepared to provide an honorarium of $400 for the six-session class, with round-trip travel between your residence and the class site also reimbursed at $.56 per mile. Please track your mileage by recording the odometer reading on the NIC Travel Reimbursement Form at the start and conclusion of your travel.

All teachers are expected to attend an Orientation Session prior to teaching their first class. The purpose of this session is not to teach teachers how to teach, but rather to introduce you to the curriculum we have designed specifically for these classes. Even if your home church has specifically requested you to teach their class, and even if you have taught for the SSL program before, you will need to attend this session in order for your class to be considered part of the "Who Is My Neighbor?" program.

In turn, we will provide each host church with a teacher's guidebook containing a copy of the curriculum and a collection of forms to assist you in your work, a student handbook, and a kit of teaching materials for use in the classroom. These materials are for your use as you teach the class, and will remain with the church or move to another church when your class is completed. At the conclusion of your six-week series, please be sure to leave the curriculum notebook and the toolkit in the church office at your host site, or deliver them to a member of the Task Force.

At the beginning of each class meeting, please check the weekly spreadsheet in your notebook. Complete the attendance roster, perform the weekly tasks listed, and return the sheet to the email address on the spreadsheet. You may fill it in digitally, or you may print it out, fill it in by hand, and scan and email the spreadsheet. This needs to be done within 24 hours after each lesson.

We are also counting on you to help us improve the curriculum. We need feedback! While we ask you not to make major changes in the classroom, and not to skip over any portion of the lesson plans, we do want to hear from you which activities are successful and which need to be modified, and in what way. That's the only way in which we will perfect this program for maximum effectiveness. An online survey via Survey Monkey will be sent to you weekly. We require this to be completed within 24 hours of each week's class meeting.

Qualities we are seeking

- Bachelor's degree or equivalent, or above
- Fluency in both Spanish and English, and excellent linguistic skills
- Excellent people skills
- Professionalism and cultural sensitivity
- Commitment to our objectives and our philosophy
- Compassion
- Commitment to Christian values as understood by the UMC
- Attendance at all six classes, with all materials and room environment fully prepared
- Organizational skills
- Access to Internet and email (check daily!)
- Dependable transportation
- Creativity
- Flexibility
- Willingness to learn along with us as we test and improve the curriculum

Memorandum of Understanding
Teacher and SSL Program

This document is for teachers in the Spanish as a Second Language program of the Northern Illinois Conference of the United Methodist Church. It is meant to guide them through the goals of the classes and the commitments of each party. In cases where "we" is used, it refers to the Spanish as a Second Language work group. Where "you" is used, it refers to the teacher of the Spanish language class.

Our goals

I. Language introduction. This course is to introduce non-Spanish speaking students to the Spanish language, with a focus on language used in a Christian worship context. We expect some religious language to be a part of our teaching.

II. Cultural awareness and sensitivity. We also invite an awareness of possible attitudes and biases towards those who may not speak English.

III. Consistency in teaching. Our teaching terms are designed to be six weeks in length, with 6 two-hour classes taught during those six weeks. Some churches may opt for a modified schedule, such as every day for five days, adjusting the class length as necessary to cover the entire curriculum.

IV. Flexibility for students. With consistent classes, we believe in allowing students the flexibility to attend one session in one location and to take the next session in another location (or even at a later term).

V. Teacher quality and support. We believe in supporting our teachers with curriculum and orientation to that curriculum. We will have one teacher and an SSL Local Church Ambassador from the host church. Wherever possible, one of those will be a native speaker of the Spanish language. This is to encourage students to feel free to engage in conversation with native speakers.

VI. A challenging, high quality curriculum. We hope this curriculum allows students to walk away feeling they have learned much about the Spanish language. As this curriculum is developed, revisions are expected and welcomed. However, to ensure high quality and consistent teaching, revisions need to occur at higher level than the individual classroom.

Our commitment to you

I. Tools for your work. We will give you the curriculum to teach, with a minimum need for preparation. We will also include a "Teacher's toolkit" of materials related to the curriculum. These items must be returned to the Conference at the conclusion of your six classes. Any additional materials you wish to purchase will be at your own expense, and they will remain your property.

II. Training. We want to train you to teach this curriculum. We will hold an orientation session where you will be introduced to the curriculum. You are required to attend the training before you will be permitted to begin teaching. We will not be able to reimburse time or travel for this orientation session. We will be able to answer your questions and engage your initial feedback.

III. Classroom support. We will enlist the help of an SSL Local Church Ambassador. This person is meant to be a volunteer laboring with you to support the work that you do. He or she will follow your lead on how best to engage the classroom, will be present in the classroom for most of the class period, and will assist with logistical tasks such as dividing the class into teams or handing out materials.

IV. On-site support. This same SSL Local Church Ambassador will help with welcoming and logistical details at each site. That includes any audio-visual support, providing "hospitality" items, setting out a basket to receive voluntary donations, completing weekly reports, and greeting you and the students.

V. Stipend Support. We understand that teaching this course is a sacrifice of your time. We consider it a ministry and a labor of love. However, we are prepared to provide an honorarium of $400 for the class (approximately $30 per hour), with round-trip travel between your residence and the class site also reimbursed at $.56 per mile, up to a maximum of $50 for travel. Please track your mileage by listing the odometer reading at the start and conclusion of your travel, and submit your request for reimbursement at the end of the series using the NIC Travel Reimbursement Form sheet in your curriculum notebook.

Your commitment to us

I. Attend the teacher orientation session. We cannot provide consistent instruction at all sites and in all classrooms without this orientation session time.

II. Teach the curriculum you have. We understand that every teacher will emphasize certain points in a curriculum differently, creating a lively, engaging class that everyone enjoys. However, we discourage developing an alternate curriculum or modifying significantly the curriculum we have. Remember that we do encourage consistent teaching. We welcome feedback on the curriculum.

III. Work with the SSL Local Church Ambassador. We encourage you to work with your SSL Local Church Ambassador as a colleague who will help you in this ministry work. You should stay in weekly communication with your SSL Local Church Ambassador.

IV. Be present. Please be at each class and teach each class lesson. You should arrive at least 20 minutes prior to the scheduled start time in order to prepare the room and materials. We encourage you to be present to your students, answering their questions and engaging them in learning.

Special note about missing a class: If there is some reasonable, unexpected cause for not being able to make a class, please notify your SSL Local Church Ambassador as soon as possible. We will be unable to provide a stipend or reimbursement for any missed class. If you are able to arrange for a substitute, the substitute will receive the honorarium and mileage for that week. The commitment to "be present" is so important to us that we may elect to replace a teacher for any failure to live up to this commitment. The Spanish as a Second Language trainers will be solely responsible for determining when that might need to occur.

V. Be positive and creative. You are invited to engage in a unique opportunity. We hope you will enjoy your time and let that positive energy exude from you as you teach.

To be signed at the teacher orientation:

_____ Date: _____
Teacher, Spanish as a Second Language Course

_____ Date: _____
Teacher trainer

Teacher Toolkit

To get your teachers started and to encourage fun and creativity on their part, we suggest providing your teachers with a Teacher Toolkit. With donations, most items in the Toolkit can be free, or can be purchased at a dollar store. Here's what we recommend:

- Two flyswatters (needed for the game of SWAT, which is usually very popular among class participants)

- A pack of blank paper (recycled office paper blank on one side will do the job)

- A roll of painter's (masking) tape (useful for drawing lines on the floor, taping lightweight notes or pictures to the wall without marring the walls, and so on)

- A pack of colored construction paper (for learning colors or whatever else you can think of)

- A pack of 3x5 index cards (used in Lesson 4, and anywhere else you think they might be useful)

- A "stress ball" (squeezy ball), any shape or color. (Every teacher should have one of these. They are great for "tossing" games. Perhaps someone in your community would like to donate some. We have used balls, hearts, hard hats, police cars--all squeezy toys from local companies, fire and police departments, and hospitals--and even crabs, which began their life as an advertisement for a conference in Baltimore.)

Most churches can supply items such as crayons or colored pencils; a whiteboard, chalkboard, or large easel; dry erase markers; and photocopies. Alternatively, you may be able to obtain these items through donation as well. What a great way to let the community know what you are doing!

Host Site
SSL Local Church Ambassador Checklist

NIC Spanish as a Second Language Class

Thank you for agreeing to serve as the SSL Local Church Ambassador for the NIC Spanish classes to be held at your church. Below are the responsibilities and commitments of the SSL Local Church Ambassador from the host congregation. In essence, you are the host for this site. We ask you to take these tasks seriously and fulfill them as you would fulfill the responsibilities of hosting in your own home:

❏ Well in advance, make sure all members of your congregation are aware of the class and its purpose, and build support and excitement for it throughout your congregation.

❏ Beginning several weeks ahead, make use of the online materials such as posters, flyers, ads, and bulletin inserts to publicize the classes. You will be sent a link to these.

❏ Take a few minutes at the beginning of the first class to introduce yourself, and also introduce the participants to the church: location of restrooms, refreshments, nursery if relevant, elevators, etc.

❏ Place a donation basket in the room, with the table tent flyer you have been given beside it. Thank the participants for registering, and explain that any donations above and beyond the registration fee are welcome and will help to defray the expenses of the program, including the teachers' honoraria. Donations are completely voluntary. Any money thus collected will be sent to a special fund of the conference for this purpose. Clarify the purpose of the donation basket to the participants.

❏ Please ask all participants to silence and store their electronic devices. Use of cell phones during class is proven to be distracting.

❏ On the day of each class meeting, place signs at church entrances and other critical points, so participants and visitors can find the entrance, room, restrooms, and whatever else they may need while they are at your site.

❏ On class days, unlock outside and inside doors as needed. Turn on lights, turn on heat or air if needed.

❏ Make sure the room is set up as requested by the teachers, insofar as your site is able to vary room setup. The teachers will let you know what they need. Please do everything possible to hold the class in the largest room available: preferably, a room large enough to hold 20 people with additional room to move around in. The sanctuary is a fine choice if that is the best option available.

❏ Have coffee, tea, water, and light snacks available for class participants.

❏ Prepare a registration table every week, with name tags for participants, an attendance roster, donation basket, and a "Technology-Free Zone" sign. Wear a name tag yourself to identify yourself as the go-to person in case of a problem.

❏ Be present in the classroom while the class is going on, to address any issues that may come up. You are a member of the class, so please participate fully.

❏ Thank participants for coming.

❏ After the class, participants will help return the classroom into its normal state and clean up their papers, but please ensure that this is properly done.

❏ Clean up beverages and return items to their place.

❏ Turn off lights, turn off heat or air if used.

❏ Please count any donations left in the basket, secure the money until the series of classes is over, and email your weekly attendance and donation spreadsheet to Rev. Michael Mann at mmann@umcnic.org.

❏ When the series is over, send all donations clearly marked "for SSL" to Rev. Michael Mann, Northern Illinois Conference, Program Office, 217 Division Street, Elgin, IL 60120.

THANK YOU FOR HOSTING!

Teacher´s Manual

How Do People Learn a Language?

First, we begin to understand.
Second, we start talking.
Third, we begin to read.
And only last, we learn how to write.

This is true of our native language, but also of any new language we learn. Keep the above in mind as you teach, and also the three important ideas below. If your students ever feel discouraged because they think they aren't learning fast enough, remind them:

- We have to *hear* a new word between *30* and *100* times before our brain can remember it and claim it as our own.
- We can only absorb and remember seven new things at a time, at most.
- Words don't correspond one-to-one to other words. Words correspond to ideas!

Where to go if you need help with this curriculum or suggestions for how to convey the ideas included here:
Ruth Cassel Hoffman: rch@language-resources.com or Maria Wilcox: virtualspanish1@gmail.com

Lesson 1

La familia

Linguistic objectives: Become familiar with the sounds of Spanish. Begin to understand a few words. Build students' confidence in their own ability to learn, understand, and speak Spanish. Introduce the following vocabulary: **hola, me llamo/se llama, pase, siéntese, es/son, mamá, papá, hermano/a, esposo/a, hijo/a, abuelo/a, tengo/tiene, numbers 1-12, vecino/a, sí, no, ¿y usted?, amor, paz, corazón.**

Cultural objectives: What is "Hispanic" or "Latino" culture? How do Spanish-speakers in the US prefer to identify themselves? Where is Spanish spoken throughout the world?

Materials needed:
>   whiteboard, markers
>   pictures of family (photos, clip art, pictures cut out from magazines, etc.)
>   roll of masking tape
>   blank paper
>   drawing materials (crayons, colored pencils, or markers)
>   large flash cards of numbers 1-12
>   (optional) dowel, walking stick, cane, or yardstick
>   two flyswatters
>   words for *Yo tengo gozo, gozo* and for *Enviado soy de Dios* (ask your SSL Local Church Ambassador to make copies for the class)

- (7 minutes) Open with prayer. Explain that in this series of classes, they will learn to understand and say about 100 words, and will be able to recognize more words than that. Tell them that the theme of the class is "Who Is My Neighbor?" and that you will be helping them learn how to be good neighbors to their Spanish-speaking coworkers, neighbors, and people they meet. Tell them that the last class will include a Communion service in Spanish and a potluck meal, both of which will be an integral part of the learning experience.

- (5 minutes) Greetings and introductions:
  - Hola.
  - Me llamo ____, ¿y usted?
  - Don't make the students reply in Spanish, just say their own name.

- (6 minutes) First commands: Take students into the hallway or outside the room, and have them knock on the door one by one or in small groups, varying the commands as needed. Use gestures to illustrate the following commands:
  - ¡Hola! ¡Pase(n)! Siénte(n)se aquí! [ADAPTATION FOR OTHER-ABLED PARTICIPANTS: Have them use the "two-finger person" on the palm of their hand or a tabletop to imitate actions such as standing, sitting, or walking.]

- (15 minutes) Use large photos, clip art, or flash cards of individual family members and tape them to a surface, or draw the heads one by one on the whiteboard as you introduce them. Use "family tree" format to help them visualize the relationships.
  - Es mi mamá. Ella se llama _____.
  - Es mi papá. Él se llama _____.
  - Es mi esposo/a. Él/Ella se llama _____.
  - Es mi hijo. Él se llama _____.
  - Es mi hija. Ella se llama _____.
  - Son mis abuelos. Ellos se llaman _____ y _____.
  - Son mis hermanos, ____ y _____.
  - Es mi hermana _____.

- (15 minutes) Give paper and crayons to students. Invite students to draw their own family. Invite them to respond to your questions. Ask 2-3 questions of each student, and hold up papers so everyone can see where you are pointing.

○ ¿Es su mamá, ¿sí? ¿Cómo se llama ella? etc.

○ Allow one-word answers: mamá, sí, no.

- (10 minutes) Introduce numbers 1-12, using large flashcards. Set out flash-cards in a large circle on the floor, making a clock. Don't say "This is how we tell time" or "This is a clock" or "This is how we count"; just let them see what you are doing and interpret it on their own. Invite students to make a circle around the flashcards on the floor, so all can see well. If you wish, use a yardstick, dowel, walking cane, or other stick to point to each card. Dangle your watch or show a clock to the class, then walk around the clock and point to each number in order:

  o Es la una. Son las dos, etc.

  ○ Then have students point to numbers as you say the time. Don't make them say the time, just have them point. Any students who already know the numbers can say them as a group.

  ○ Emphasize **dos/diez/doce**, so students can hear the difference. They all sound alike to a beginner. Same for **cinco/seis/siete** and for **uno/once**. If you are a native speaker, this statement may seem ridiculous, but it is true. To teach your native language effectively, you must think like a beginner.

- (10 minutes) Play SWAT: Divide group into two teams. (The teams do not have to be even in number.) Have each team line up behind each other facing the whiteboard. Give the first person on each team a flyswatter.

  ○ Using the pictures of family members that are already on the whiteboard and numbers 1-12 that you have scattered among the pictures, call out a word (**hermano, abuela, tres, etc.**).

  ○ The holder of the flyswatter must run to the board and swat the appropriate picture on the board. [ADAPTATION FOR OTHER-ABLED PARTICIPANTS: Station the swatter-holders close to the whiteboard so they don't have to run. Or assign partners within teams, to work together.]

  ○ Tell participants to hold their flyswatter in place after swatting, so that you can see who got there first! If you wish, keep score so you can determine the winning team.

- (15 minutes) Cultural Insight lesson (in English): The Cultural Insight lessons are located in the Culture chapter of this Curriculum, beginning on page 24. They do not need to be delivered in any particular order, but we have indicated a recommended order with each Insight. Please read the Guide for Teachers and the Cultural Tidbits in that section for guidance in how to use the Cultural Insights and for resources and information. Recommended Cultural Insight for this lesson: Self-Identity.

GIVE A BATHROOM/COFFEE BREAK (10 minutes) AFTER ABOUT ONE HOUR OF CLASSTIME.

- (10 minutes) Review family members and numbers, using the following statements and questions as examples:

  ○ En mi familia, tengo ___ personas.

  ○ Tengo una mamá y un papá.

  ○ Tengo dos hermanos: un hermano y una hermana.

  ○ ¿En su familia, tiene cuatro/diez/once personas?

  ○ Don't expect full sentences. Use questions that can be answered with a number, a single word, **sí** or **no**, or even by holding up fingers. Ask leading questions to guide nonspeakers to understand.

  ○ Note that we are intentionally using *tener* rather than *hay*, because the song at the end of this lesson uses *tengo*.

- (10 minutes) Song ("I have a joy, joy, joy, joy down in my heart..."). If you don't sing, ask someone in the class to lead the singing. Teach the words by speaking them first and using gestures, then add the melody. Give out the word sheet after singing the song.

  Yo tengo gozo, gozo en mi corazón (spoken: ¿Dónde?)
  En mi corazón, en mi corazón.
  Yo tengo gozo, gozo en mi corazón, (spoken: ¿Dónde?)
  En mi corazón, ¡sí, sí!

  Yo tengo paz de Cristo, paz de Cristo, en mi corazón, (spoken: ¿Dónde?)
  En mi corazón, en mi corazón.
  Yo tengo paz de Cristo, paz de Cristo, en mi corazón, (spoken: ¿Dónde?)
  En mi corazón, ¡sí, sí!

Yo tengo amor de Cristo, amor de Cristo, en mi corazón, (spoken:
   ¿Dónde?)
En mi corazón, en mi corazón.
Yo tengo amor de Cristo, amor de Cristo, en mi corazón, (spoken:
   ¿Dónde?)
En mi corazón, ¡sí, sí!
(On this verse, you will have to elide "tengo amor" and "Cristo, amor".)

- (6-7 minutes) Conversaciones entre vecinos: Explain that you are each going to have a conversation in Spanish with your neighbor, *su vecino*. Group them by twos or threes, and with a hand on the shoulder of each member of a group, say: **Ustedes son vecinos**. Do this for each group. Tell them (in English) that they should use this time to say whatever words they can remember in Spanish, and draw pictures or point to people or objects to help indicate that they understand the meaning. They can help each other get the words right. It's okay if all they can do is take turns counting to each other. Just try to speak only Spanish. The goal is to reflect back the words they have learned, to demonstrate comprehension, and to build confidence in saying Spanish words out loud.

- (5 minutes) Close by reading the story of the Good Samaritan in Spanish, and by singing *Enviado soy de Dios*. Tell them that by the end of the six-week series, they will be able to understand all the keywords of this important story, and of the song. Give out the song sheet with the music for them to sing from, since this song is more complicated than *Yo tengo gozo, gozo*.

- Say **gracias** to students and dismiss with prayer.

Lesson 2

Mi vecino es...

Linguistic objectives: Build on comprehension. Elicit one-word answers to simple questions. Introduce the following vocabulary: **grande, alto/a, chico/a (or pequeño/a), mediano/a, ¿cuánto(a)(s)?, pelo, rubio/a, canas, gris, negro/a, pelirrojo/a, calvo/a, serio/a, chistoso/a, feliz, triste, amable, ¿quién?** and the words to *Cristo me ama*.

Cultural objectives: Understanding the use of "double" last names among Spanish-speakers.

Materials needed:
    dry-erase markers
    Cutout hearts and mouths (lips curved up, lips curved down, lips in a straight line, lips open in a laughing shape); have 4-5 of each for students to pass around; make them larger than life-size. Cut them out of red paper plates or red construction paper.
    Words for Cristo me ama (give out after singing)
    (for small classes) index cards, or a large number of small objects such as plastic spoons
    words for Cristo me ama (ask your SSL Local Church Ambassador to make copies for the class)

- (5 minutes) Greet students as they arrive, using the words learned last time. Open with prayer.

- (10 minutes) Review family members and numbers while teaching **¿cuántos? ¿cuántas?**:

  - Say: **En mi familia, tengo ___ personas: mi mamá, mi esposo, mis dos hijos**.... Count on your fingers to demonstrate.

  - **En su familia, ¿cuántas personas tiene?** (Help the student enumerate who they are.) Ask various individuals. [Note: never go around the room in order. Always mix it up so the participants can't predict when they will be called on.]

  - **¿En esta sala (gesture), ¿cuántas personas tenemos?**

- (8 minutes) Number game (for large classes): Tell students you will call out a number. They must arrange themselves in groups of that number. If there are not enough people to fill out a group, the last few should group themselves and hold up the number of fingers lacking to make up the total number. If you call 5 and there are 20 people present, there should be 4 groups of 5 people. If there are only 18 people present, the last 3 should group themselves and hold up 2 fingers.

  - Alternate game (for small classes): Scatter plastic spoons or index cards all over the floor. Tell students you will call out a number, and each student much pick up the appropriate number of items, holding them high to display them. They may compare with each other to make sure everyone has the correct number. Drop the items on the floor again and call out another number. Continue until all seem comfortable with the numbers you have taught so far.

- (10 minutes) Grande, alto, chico, mediano:

  - Draw a large, a medium, and a small house on the board. As you draw, say **Esta casa es grande...Esta casa es chica...Esta casa es mediana**. Point in turn to each house and ask the group, ¿Es una casa grande? Es una casa chica? Make the answer sometimes sí, sometimes no.

  - Draw a tall stick figure and a short one. As you draw, say **Esta persona es alta. Esta persona es chica**. Repeat the house questions for the people.

  - Point to the tallest person in the class. Ask **¿_____ es alto/a o chico/a?** Now the shortest person: **¿_____ es alto/a o chico/a?** Ask about various other people, varying the gender so they can hear and practice both forms, including yourself. Point to yourself and ask **¿Soy yo alto/a o chico/a?** Line students up by height and point to each: **alto/a, mediano/a, chico/a**.

- (15 minutes) Draw a series of heads on the board. Use different colored markers to give hair to each head.
  - ○ Point to the figures in turn and say **Es mi amigo/a. Él es rubio (ella es rubia)**. Do the same for **pelirrojo/a**. Say **él tiene pelo negro, ella tiene canas, él está calvo** .
  - ○ Identify hair color for each person in the room.
  - ○ Hand the markers to a student and ask him/her: **Dibuje una mamá pelirroja**.Another student: **Dibuje un abuelo con canas**. And so on. Keep it moving rapidly.
  - ○ As soon as a few have demonstrated the ability to understand your commands, expand the command for the next few: **Dibuje un hermano alto con pelo negro. Dibuje una abuela chica con canas.**
  - ○ Note: It is fine to use different terminology for hair color if you wish. These words vary widely by Hispanic culture and no one version is correct.

BREAK TIME! (10 minutes)

- (15 minutes) **Serio, chistoso, feliz, triste, amable** (**ser** and **estar**), and **¿quién?**
  - ○ Begin by explaining in English that there are two ways to say the verb to be in Spanish. One is usually for things that are permanent characteristics, like being tall or short. The other is for things that are changeable, like your mood today. (If someone asks about the weather, tell them that's another story, to be saved for later.) Talk briefly about the difference between being in a mood vs. having a certain personality (**ser** and **estar**). Don't go into detail, just state the rule again succinctly. Tell students that the important thing at this level is to recognize that these two verbs exist so they won't be taken by surprise, not to understand all the nuances and rules for knowing which one to use.
  - ○ Hand out mouths and hearts to class members. Keep one set for yourself.
  - ○ Hold a smiling mouth in front of your face and say **¡Estoy feliz!** Switch to a sad mouth and say: **¡Estoy triste!** Switch back and forth several times, repeating the Spanish. Point out that sometimes you are **triste**, and sometimes **feliz**, so you say **estoy**.
  - ○ Ask **¿Quién está feliz?** and look for people who are holding the smiling mouths. Have them hold the mouths in front of their faces. Same with **triste**. Point out that **está** is for talking about someone else, not yourself, and is a partner to **estoy**.

○ Put on a serious mouth. Say **Soy una persona seria**. Put on the laughing mouth: **Soy una persona chistosa**. Ask: **¿Quién es serio? ¿Quién es chistoso?** Have students look for the ones with the serious or laughing mouths, and identify them by pointing, saying their name, or (if they can) saying _____ **es chistoso**. Don't force full sentences. At this point they are doing well if they understand and react appropriately. Indicate that these are personality traits, so now you are saying es.

○ Hold a heart in front of your chest, and say, **Soy una persona amable**. Ask about various others: **¿Es _____ una persona amable?** Soy is partner to es.

- (5 minutes) Song: *Cristo me ama* (Jesus Loves Me):

> Cristo me ama, bien lo sé,
>
> En la Biblia dice así.
>
> Todos niños son de Él,
>
> Él es nuestro amigo fiel.
>
> Cristo me ama,
>
> Cristo me ama,
>
> Cristo me ama,
>
> La Biblia dice así.

[Give out the song sheet after they have sung the song. Point out resemblance between ama *and* amable, *that they are related. Also point out that God's love is permanent, so we say es and son instead of* está *and* están.*]*

- (15 minutes) Cultural insight (in English): Recommended insight for this lesson: Names.

- (10 minutes) Conversación con mi vecino:

○ Group them in twos and threes as last week. Again, have them recite all the Spanish words they can to each other, helping each other. To give it a little structure, invite them to try to describe each other or their family members out loud. Teacher circulates and listens. Encourage them not to try to use full sentences if they're not ready yet. Single-word utterances are fine. For example: Papá: alto, serio, canas.

- Invite students to get out their song sheet for *Enviado soy de Dios*. Close with *Enviado soy de Dios* and prayer.

Lesson 3

Me gusta, no me gusta, ¡qué pena!

Linguistic objectives: Name colors. Learn how to express likes and dislikes, empathy and shared joy. Base words: **el color, rojo, naranja, amarillo, verde, azul, violeta, gris, café, blanco, negro, el campo, la primavera, el pájaro, afuera, viene, venga, el arco iris, mire, vemos, veo, escuche, ponga, por eso, el amor, (no) me gusta(n), el gallo, la gallina, el pollo, cante, la caja, ¡qué pena!**

Cultural objectives: Understanding differing concepts of personal space and touch. How do we greet each other? Does everybody hug and kiss?

Materials needed:

> Computer to show video of song (find online)
> Handout of words for *De colores*
> Pictures: rainbow, bird, rooster, hen, chick, field/meadow
> Multi-colored pack of construction paper

- (5 minutes) Greet participants. Open with prayer.

- (10 minutes) Introduce *De colores* song:
  - ❍ Play video.
  - ❍ Do not hand out the words yet, but point out 1) that the words are on the screen, 2) that you will give them the words in a little while, and 3) that you will be teaching and practicing the new words later in this lesson.
  - ❍ Replay video, pausing to point out words that they may already be familiar with or be able to guess. Have them show you with appropriate actions what those words mean.
  - ❍ Replay. Invite students to sing along with the parts that they have "caught".

- (15 minutes) Introduce new vocabulary, using commands and words already learned whenever possible:
  - ❍ Use commands to teach **venga, mire, escuche, cante, ponga, el campo, el pájaro, el arco iris, el gallo, la gallina, el pollito**. Demonstrate each command before asking students to perform the action. Do not translate. Show them what each command means by performing it yourself. Mix it up, do not always issue the commands in the same order or to the class members in the same order, and give commands sometimes to individuals and sometimes to groups. Example: _____, **cante.** ____, **escuche a** ____. **Ponga el arco iris en la caja. Mire el pájaro**. Be sure you don't ask anyone to perform a command that you have not already demonstrated.
  - ❍ Add **el amor.** One way to illustrate this is with the American Sign Language shortcut for "I love you" (the ILY handshape). They will have no trouble understanding the word anyway.
  - ❍ Don't forget to incorporate previously-learned vocabulary into the mix of commands: the names of family members, numbers, descriptions of people.

- (10 minutes) Introduce the colors
  - ❍ Use commands with sheets of colored construction paper to teach the colors. Give active commands such as **Ponga el rojo en el arco iris. Ponga el azul en el rojo. Mire el amarillo.** As before, demonstrate each command containing a new word before asking any participant to perform the command. Keep this segment fast-paced and short. It is not the most important part of the lesson.

- (10 minutes) Practice the colors
  - ○ Again, keep this segment fast-paced and short. It is not the most important part of the lesson.
  - ○ Scatter the entire pack of construction paper all over the floor, mixing up the colors. Enlist help from class members to expedite this task. Tell students that when you name a color, they should each find a sheet of that color and stand on it. If there are more participants than sheets of a given color, they should cluster with someone else who has found the correct color. Give them a moment to look around and verify that they are all in the right place, then call out another color.
  - ○ When you have called out all the colors, tell students that now they are to pick up all sheets of the color you call out. Have them return the sheets to you in piles divided by color. You can assign a small group to pick up each color; this way the job will go faster.
  - ○ [ALTERNATIVE GAME FOR SMALL GROUPS: Play SWAT. Tape the construction paper (one of each color you are teaching) to the whiteboard or wall.]

COFFEE/BATHROOM BREAK (10 minutes)

- (15 minutes) Review song: *De colores*
  - ○ Hand out the words to the song.
  - ○ Read them out loud to the students. Ignore the little words, but translate any words the participants ask about. Don't explain points of grammar at this level. (When they ask "why?" the answer is usually "because". Period.) If they seem to be comfortable, invite them to read along with you as a group. Don't make anyone read solo.
  - ○ Play the song once more, and invite students to sing along if they wish.

- (10 minutes) **Conversaciones con los vecinos**:
  - ○ Tell the class a (brief) sad story (in English, but include some Spanish words that they know). It can be humorous (a trivial disaster, for example, such as spilling a whole box of paper-clips, or having the dog eat your cookies, or dropping a birthday cake on the floor). End your story with **¡Ay, qué pena!** Have them repeat the response as a group, several times.

○ Break them into small groups, or go around the circle. Have them take turns telling each other sad stories of a similar sort, and respond to each other with **¡Ay, qué pena!** and making a sad facial expression.

- (15 minutes) Likes and dislikes:

  ○ Explain that saying "I like" and "I don't like" has to be flipped in Spanish, compared to the sentence structure in English. Compare the Spanish construction to "It is pleasing to me" in English. Point out that in English, we also have to change the sentence if we like or dislike more than one thing: "Bananas are pleasing to me".

  ○ Write the four forms on the whiteboard: **Me gusta, no me gusta, me gustan, no me gustan**. Point out that if you are talking about liking more than one thing, there is an extra letter on the verb, just as we change is and are in English. Have them practice as a group saying each form a couple of times.

  ○ Tell them this game is better than Facebook, because there is a "Like" button and a "Dislike" button. Start with a few items in English. Ask "Do you like yellow? Do you like bananas? Do you like car accidents? Do you like broccoli? Do you like to sing? Have them answer all together in Spanish: **¡Sí, me gusta(n)!** or **¡No, no me gusta(n)!** Make them be enthusiastic and use happy or disgusted faces. Invite them to make thumbs-up or thumbs-down gestures with each response.

  ○ Switch to asking the questions in Spanish, and use words that the students know: **¿Le gustan las familias? Le gusta el rojo? Le gustan los gallos? Le gustan los niños? Le gusta la primavera?** and so on.

- (15 minutes) Cultural insight (in English): Recommended insight for this lesson: Personal space/touch.

- (5 minutes) Invite students to get out their song sheets for *Enviado soy de Dios*. Close with the hymn and a simple prayer in Spanish.

Lesson 4

El buen samaritano y el gran mandamiento

Linguistic objectives: To learn the vocabulary of the Great Commandment, and to begin using full sentences in Spanish. To lay the groundwork for telling our own stories in Spanish, however brief. Introduce the following vocabulary: **ama, el Señor, la fuerza, la mente, el alma, el prójimo, todo/a, ti mismo, quién**, numbers 13-20.

Cultural objectives: What is "hora latina"? Understanding differing concepts of time, punctuality, and hospitality.

Materials needed:
> Worksheet on Great Commandment (see page 41)
> Two sets of index cards for the Great Commandment (see page 42)
> Two flyswatters for SWAT
> Markers, eraser, whiteboard

- (5 minutes) Greet participants. Open with prayer.

- (20 minutes) Review of vocabulary. Play SWAT:

  o Write an assortment of words they have learned in random locations on the whiteboard. Include words from all three previous lessons. Speak each word out loud as you write it.

  o Play SWAT.

  o Erase the words they seem to know well. Write another assortment of words they have learned, keeping the words they had trouble with.

  o Play another round of SWAT.

- (20 minutes) Meeting the Good Samaritan in Spanish:

  o Read aloud the story of the Good Samaritan in English. Use a recent translation such as the CEB.

  o Assign roles (in Spanish) to class members: the traveler, the bandits (as many as you like!), the priest, the Levite, the Samaritan, the innkeeper. (If the class seems to enjoy silliness, you can even assign someone to be the donkey.)

Lucas 10:30-37

30 Jesús entonces le contestó:

–Un hombre iba por el camino de Jerusalén a Jericó, y unos bandidos lo asaltaron y le quitaron hasta la ropa; lo golpearon y se fueron, dejándolo medio muerto. 31Por casualidad, un sacerdote pasaba por el mismo camino; pero al verlo, dio un rodeo y siguió adelante. 32 También un levita llegó a aquel lugar, y cuando lo vio, dio un rodeo y siguió adelante. 33 Pero un hombre de Samaria que viajaba por el mismo camino, al verlo, sintió compasión. 34 Se acercó a él, le curó las heridas con aceite y vino, y le puso vendas. Luego lo subió en su propia cabalgadura, lo llevó a un alojamiento y lo cuidó. 35 Al día siguiente, el samaritano sacó el equivalente al salario de dos días, se lo dio al dueño del alojamiento y le dijo: "Cuide a este hombre, y si gasta usted algo más, yo se lo pagaré cuando vuelva." 36 Pues bien, ¿cuál de esos tres te parece que se hizo prójimo del hombre asaltado por los bandidos?

37 El maestro de la ley contestó:

–El que tuvo compasión de él.

Jesús le dijo:

–Pues ve y haz tú lo mismo.

○ Now read the story again, in Spanish this time, but slowly, and giving the "actors" time to play their roles. Use a modern translation because of the simpler language. Here is the text in the Dios Habla Hoy (DHH) version:

○ Have the students act out the story as you read it, slowly, in Spanish. They can mime or gesture the speaking parts. Don't ask them to talk. The point is to practice understanding spoken Spanish, even when it contains words they aren't familiar with.

- (10 minutes) New vocabulary for the Great Commandment:

  ○ Read to students in English. They can probably recite it along with you.

  ○ Read it to them in Spanish: **Ama al Señor tu Dios con todo tu corazón, con toda tu alma, con todas tus fuerzas, y con toda tu mente, y ama a tu prójimo como a ti mismo.**

  ○ Point out words they already know: **Señor, Dios** (they know **adios**, which is commending the departing person to God), **corazón**. Show **la fuerza** by showing strong biceps. Point out that **la mente** is related to *mental* in English (but not to Mentos candy!). Translate **el alma** for them. Point out that **el prójimo** means the same as **el vecino**—it's the person who is in proximity to you. Also point out the difference between **todo** and **toda**.

  ○ Read the Great Commandment again.

BREAK (10 minutes)

- (20 minutes) Learning to recite the Great Commandment:

  ○ Recite the Great Commandment again in Spanish.

  ○ Give them the attached worksheet. Invite them to work in pairs or threes to fill in the blanks, using the words supplied on the worksheet.

  ○ Check results with class as a whole. Make sure everyone understands and was able to recognize the missing words.

  ○ Hand out the index cards, previously prepared, in random order to participants. Have each one read the phrase he/she is holding, in order, to recite the Great Commandment.

  ○ Have them pass their cards to another participant. Repeat the reading aloud in order.

  ○ Repeat a third time. Collect the cards.

- ○ Invite a class member to begin reciting the commandment from the beginning. When/if that person gets stuck, have someone else continue until stuck, and so on.

- ○ Hand out the other set of index cards (one word on each). Have the students stand up and arrange themselves in order. Remind them that some words appear more than once, so they will have to find the right places. Have each recite his/her word, trying to make it smooth. Have them recite all together.

- (10 minutes) **¿Quién?** (Review old vocabulary):

  - ○ Ask questions of the class. The questions should be about themselves. Examples:

    - ☆ ¿quién tiene dos hermanos?

    - ☆ ¿quién tiene una mamá y no papá?

    - ☆ ¿quién es pelirrojo?

    - ☆ ¿quién está triste?

    - ☆ ¿quién está feliz?

  - ○ Refer to previous lessons to remind yourself of what they know. Anyone may answer, giving names of people who correspond to the question, pointing to the individual(s), or pointing to themselves.

- (10 minutes) Review numbers 1-12, add numbers 13-21:

  - ○ Each person says a number, in order, 1-12. When you get to 12, start over with the next person.

  - ○ Point out the **–ce** pattern in **once** and **doce**. Say that the pattern continues with the next few numbers: **trece, catorce, quince**. Tell them then it gets easier with a little addition. Say the numbers slowly so they can hear the "math problem": **dieciséis** = 10 + 6, and so on.

  - ○ Have them count 1-21. Now have them count down from 21 to 1. Write the numbers on the board as they say them, to help them keep their place.

- (10 minutes) Cultural insight (in English): Recommended insight for this lesson: The sense of time.

- (5 minutes) Sing *Enviado soy de Dios*. Dismiss with prayer.

Worksheet: El gran mandamiento

Fill in the blanks with the words in the word basket. Each word is only used once.

Word basket

alma	ama	corazón
prójimo	Dios	tus
mismo	toda	mente

Ama al Señor tu _____ con todo tu

_____, con toda tu _____,

con todas _____ fuerzas, y con

_____ tu _____, y

_____ a tu _____ como a

ti _____.

How to prepare index cards for Lesson 4 on the Great Commandment:

Set #1 (7 cards):
Each card should have one phrase on it, divided as follows:

> Ama al Señor tu Dios
>
> con todo tu corazón
>
> con toda tu alma
>
> con todas tus fuerzas
>
> y con toda tu mente
>
> y ama a tu prójimo
>
> como a ti mismo

Set #2 (31cards):
Each card should have only one word on it, as follows:

> Ama
>
> al
>
> Señor
>
> tu
>
> Dios
>
> etc.

On both sets of cards, capitalize where it is correct to use a capital letter, but don't punctuate.

Lesson 5

Padrenuestro

Linguistic objectives: Familiarize students with the Lord's Prayer in Spanish, not to memorize it completely, but to recognize it when they hear it, and to teach the commonly-used words it contains. They should be able to pray the Lord's Prayer in Spanish with a "cheat sheet" in hand. Introduce the following vocabulary: **hacer, el mal, el bien, el amor, con, mantener, el padre, nuestro, el cielo, el nombre, el reino, la tierra, el pan, el día, perdonar, el poder, la gloria, cada, sencillo/a, la voluntad, da/dé, hoy, librar, la tentación, tuyo/a, ahora, siempre**.

Cultural objectives: Do other countries celebrate an Independence Day? When? What is the real meaning of Cinco de Mayo? Who celebrates it?

Materials needed:
> Cut out pictures from magazines: 5 pictures each of people doing good and doing harm.
> Handout with words of Lord's Prayer
> Markers, whiteboard

Note: Remind participants that there will be a shared meal in the second hour of the last class next time, and that they should bring a dish to share. Use a sign-up sheet to solicit dishes: salad, main dish, dessert, to make sure you have a reasonable assortment of food.

- (5 minutes) Greet students as they arrive, using the words learned last time. Open with prayer.

- (10 minutes) Introduce John Wesley's *Tres reglas sencillas*: practical rules for living out the Great Commandment. **No hacer el mal. Hacer el bien. Mantener el amor con Dios**. (Do no harm. Do good. Stay in love with God.)
  - ❍ Show pictures of doing good and doing harm: ask students to identify each as **el bien** or **el mal**. They can call out their answers.

- (5 minutes) Say that one of the ways we live by the Great Commandment and by the *Three Simple Rules* is by worshipping together. One of the common elements in Christian worship is the Lord's Prayer, so we will learn to say that. In the next (last) class we will learn other words relevant for worship.

- (15 minutes) Introduce Lord's Prayer vocabulary:
  - ❍ Draw quick pictures (they don't have to be beautiful!) on the whiteboard to introduce some of the vocabulary of the prayer. Say the words as you draw the pictures:
    - ☆ a cloud for **el cielo**
    - ☆ a randomly-chosen name for **tu Nombre**
    - ☆ a crown for **el reino**
    - ☆ a globe for **la tierra**
    - ☆ a loaf of bread for **nuestro pan**
    - ☆ a calendar for **cada día**
    - ☆ a stick figure falling down for **caer**
    - ☆ an arm with a biceps bump for **el poder**
    - ☆ a shining sun for **la gloria**
  - ❍ Repeat the words in a different order, while you point to the correct picture.
  - ❍ Ask volunteers to point to the right picture as you say the words. Keep it moving quickly.
  - ❍ If they are still having trouble recognizing the words, play SWAT with the pictures on the board.

BREAK (10 minutes)

- (25 minutes) Introduce the Lord's Prayer itself. We recommend this translation because it is simpler than some others:

> Padre nuestro que estás en el cielo,
> santificado sea tu Nombre,
> venga tu reino,
> hágase tu voluntad,
> en la tierra como en el cielo.
> Danos hoy nuestro pan de cada día.
> Perdona nuestras ofensas,
> como también nosotros perdonamos
> a los que nos ofenden.
> No nos dejes caer en tentación
> y líbranos del mal.
> Porque tuyo es el reino,
> tuyo es el poder,
> y tuya es la gloria,
> ahora y por siempre. Amén.

- ○ Tell them you are going to teach it backwards. (This sounds counterintuitive, so you will have to assure the students that it works. Do not let their trepidation overcome your confidence in using this effective learning technique. Show complete confidence.) Start with the LAST phrase. This will help them learn the sequence of phrases more quickly and more surely. Say the phrase several times, have the students repeat it after you, say it again, have students repeat again.

- ○ Then say the NEXT-TO-LAST phrase AND the last phrase. Have students repeat.

- ○ Continue in this fashion until they get to the beginning of the prayer.

- ○ Give the students the handout with the words of the Lord's Prayer so they can practice it at home.

- (15 minutes) Cultural insight (in English): Recommended insight for this lesson: Fiestas patrias (Independence Day).

- (10 minutes) If you finish early, review earlier lessons. Ask questions that use previously-learned vocabulary. Or have a songfest in Spanish: Sing any (or all!) of the songs they have sung: *Yo tengo gozo, gozo...*, *Cristo me ama¸ De colores, or Enviado soy de Dios*.

- (5 minutes) Dismiss by saying the Lord's Prayer together once more. REMIND PARTICIPANTS TO BRING A DISH TO SHARE NEXT TIME.

Lesson 6

Esto es mi cuerpo

Linguistic objectives: Review and use all learned vocabulary. Learn to recognize the words of the Sacrament of Holy Communion. Introduce the following vocabulary: **la cena, el cuerpo, la sangre, el pan, la copa, esto es, toma, partir (el pan), compartir, derramar, dar gracias**. Learn how to talk about food while enjoying a meal.

Cultural objectives: Learning about United Methodist Church VIM (Volunteers In Mission) projects. Preparing students to visit and participate in a Latino worship service. Experience an abbreviated Spanish-language worship service that includes communion.

Materials needed:
>   Communion elements (any bread and grape juice is permissible)
>   Picture of Last Supper (reproduction of a famous painting)

If the teacher is not an ordained elder in the United Methodist Church, there must be a Spanish-speaking clergy person participating in this class meeting, working beforehand with the teacher to incorporate the vocabulary learned. Use a round sitting arrangement with the sacraments in the center of the circle, visible to all. We will assign an elder if needed. It is important for this service to be offered correctly, following the guidelines of the United Methodist Church, and presented in fluent Spanish. It should be offered in a spirit of worship, humbly and prayerfully.

Keep this class to one hour to allow for the potluck following it.

(5 minutes) Greet students. Ensure that potluck dishes are properly kept hot or cold, as needed.

- (5 minutes) Open with Lord's Prayer in Spanish.

- (15 minutes) **La Cena** (The Last Supper):

   ○ Read the Last Supper story from Matthew 26: 26-30 to the class in English. Use the CEB version if possible.

   ○ Read again, this time in Spanish, slowly. Use gestures to help students keep their place in the text. Use a picture of the Last Supper and the actual communion elements laid out in the center of the circle to highlight and point out vocabulary items as they occur in the story.

   ○ Here is the *Dios habla hoy* translation:

Mateo 26:26-30

26 Mientras comían, Jesús tomó en sus manos el pan y, habiendo dado gracias a Dios, lo partió y se lo dio a los discípulos, diciendo:

–Tomen y coman, esto es mi cuerpo.

27 Luego tomó en sus manos una copa y, habiendo dado gracias a Dios, se la pasó a ellos, diciendo:

–Beban todos ustedes de esta copa, 28 porque esto es mi sangre, con la que se confirma la alianza, sangre que es derramada en favor de muchos para perdón de sus pecados. 29 Pero les digo que no volveré a beber de este producto de la vid, hasta el día en que beba con ustedes el vino nuevo en el reino de mi Padre.

30 Después de cantar los salmos, se fueron al Monte de los Olivos.

○ Answer any questions the participants may have about words in the story.

- (15 minutes) Cultural insight (in English): Recommended insight for this lesson is Where in the world Is VIM?

- (15 minutes) Closing: Holy Communion. Brief service in Spanish. For this purpose, the teacher and the pastor should work together to adapt the service on pages 53-55 of *Fiesta Cristiana*. A copy of this order of worship is inserted at the end of this lesson. Hand out copies to the students and allow them to follow along.

BREAK AND POTLUCK!
(Save 10 minutes at the end for dismissal)

- (10 minutes) Dismissal: Invite students to attend a Hispanic worship service the following week. Give out list of church locations offering worship in Spanish, and times of services. If this makes them nervous, suggest that several of them attend together, so as not to feel overwhelmed. They could notify the pastor in advance that they intend to worship there, so the pastor will be aware of their presence in the congregation. Close with prayer and *Enviado soy de Dios*.

Orden del culto de la Santa Comunión

(Adapted from *Fiesta Cristiana: Recursos para la adoración*, written and compiled by Joel N. Martínez and Raquel M. Martínez: Nashville, TN, Abingdon Press, 2003, p. 53-55.)

Saludo

La gracia del Señor Jesucristo sea con ustedes.
Y también contigo.
El Cristo resucitado está con nosotros.
¡Alabemos al Señor!

Invitación

Cristo nuestro Señor invita a su mesa a quienes le aman, a quienes verdadera y sinceramente se arrepienten de sus pecados y procuran vivir en paz y amor con el prójimo. Confesemos, por lo tanto, nuestro pecado delante de Dios, en presencia los unos de los otros:

Dios misericordioso, confesamos que no te hemos amado de todo corazón, y con frecuencia no hemos sido una iglesia fiel. No hemos cumplido con tu voluntad, hemos violado tu ley, nos hemos rebelado en contra de tu amor, no hemos amado a nuestro prójimo y no hemos escuchado la voz del necesitado. Perdónanos, oh Dios, te lo rogamos. Libéranos para que te sirvamos con gozo, mediante Jesucristo nuestro Señor. Amén.

Escuchen las buenas nuevas: «Dios muestra su amor para con nosotros, en que siendo aún pecadores, Cristo murió por nosotros» (Romanos 5:8). ¡En el nombre de Jesucristo son perdonados!

¡En el nombre de Jesucristo eres perdonado(a)!
Gloria a Dios. Amén.

La gran acción de gracias

Elevemos nuestros corazones y demos gracias a Dios.

Santo eres tú y bendito es tu Hijo Jesucristo, a quien ungiste con tu Espíritu para predicar buenas nuevas a los pobres, sanar a los quebrantados de corazón, proclamar libertad a los cautivos, dar vista a los ciegos, y poner en libertad a los oprimidos; para proclamar el año agradable del Señor. Jesús, el Médico divino, sanó a los enfermos, a los paralíticos, y a los cojos. Jesús, el buen Pastor, tuvo compasión de su pueblo, dio de comer a los hambrientos, dio agua viva a los sedientos y comió con los pecadores.

Oh Dios, a través de su sufrimiento y muerte nos liberaste del pecado y de la muerte y destruiste sus poderes para siempre. Levantaste de los muertos a este mismo Jesucristo que ahora reina contigo en gloria, derramaste sobre nosotros tu Santo Espíritu, e hiciste con nosotros un nuevo pacto.

En la noche que fue entregado, Jesús tomó el pan, y habiendo dado gracias, lo partió, lo dio a sus discípulos y dijo: «Tomad, comed, esto es mi cuerpo que por vosotros es partido. Haced esto en memoria de mí».

Asimismo, tomó la copa después de haber cenado y, habiendo dado gracias, la dio a sus discípulos y dijo: «Tomad de esta copa que es el nuevo pacto en mi sangre, derramada por muchos para el perdón de sus pecados. Haced esto todas las veces que la bebiereis, en memoria de mí».

Derrama tu Santo Espíritu sobre quienes estamos aquí reunidos y sobre estos dones de pan y vino; haz que sean para nosotros el cuerpo y la sangre de Cristo para que, renovados y redimidos por su sangre, seamos el cuerpo de Cristo para el mundo, hasta que Cristo venga en su victoria final y podamos todos participar del banquete celestial.

Mediante tu Hijo Jesucristo, en la unidad de Espíritu Santo, a ti sea todo honor y gloria, Dios omnipotente, ahora y siempre. Amén.

El Padrenuestro

**Padre nuestro que estás en el cielo,
santificado sea tu Nombre,
venga tu reino,**

hágase tu voluntad,
en la tierra como en el cielo.
Danos hoy nuestro pan de cada día.
Perdona nuestras ofensas,
como también nosotros perdonamos
a los que nos ofenden.
No nos dejes caer en tentación
y líbranos del mal.
Porque tuyo es el reino,
tuyo es el poder,
y tuya es la gloria,
ahora y por siempre. Amén.

Se comparten el pan y la copa

Se comparte el pan y la copa a quienes estén presentes, y se dicen estas palabras:
    N..., el cuerpo de Cristo que fue entregado por ti.
    N..., la sangre de Cristo que fue derramada por ti.

Bendición

CULTURAL INSIGHTS
Guide for Teachers

General information

The primary goals of the cultural insights lessons are to foster better understanding of those who speak Spanish as their native language and to encourage mutual respect and radical hospitality across cultural boundaries.

To this end, the cultural insights are aligned with the themes of the language lessons of the curriculum and are meant to accompany each of those lessons.

The cultural insights are designed to be short and succinct, lasting about 15 minutes. They are meant to provide generalizable cultural information and overall guidance to better understand and communicate with our Spanish-speaking neighbors. The lessons are not meant to be long discussions and debates about cultural ideals, customs or practices.

The cultural insights follow one of three general formats: 1) a cultural vignette or situation where students examine and learn about cultural assumptions behind a particular situation; 2) cultural comparisons where students compare and contrast two or more cultural practices or events; and 3) a geo-cultural lesson where students identify places and people according to a set of cultural information presented. In every lesson, the end goal is to foster better understanding of targeted, specific culture groups and learn strategies that help us better communicate with our neighbors across cultural boundaries.

Because cultural discussions are very personal and can become emotional, it is important that everyone follow a few basic rules during the lesson:

- Listen carefully to others before responding
- Always show respect when speaking to and about other people
- Only speak from your own experiences—use "I" words

Procedures for cultural insights

Cultural vignette/situation:

1. Post or read out loud the situation to the students

2. Ask students to get together in pairs and try to answer the following questions about the vignette/situation:

   - What is the dilemma or conflict here?
   - What cultural assumptions do you think are operating behind what is happening?
   - What cultural information/understanding may be needed to help the people involved to problem solve and show radical hospitality toward each other?

3. Give each pair about 5-7 minutes to discuss

4. Conduct class debrief by asking some students to share their ideas

5. Show the explanation to students by explaining the answers to the questions.

6. Optional: end with a short prayer related to the lesson, asking God to help us better understand each other as we work on becoming better neighbors to one another through mutual respect and cross-cultural understanding.

Cultural comparison/Venn diagram:

1. Ask students to generate/brainstorm answers to a cultural practice that is familiar to them that is the main topic of the lesson

2. Pose the question: "How do you think this same thing is practiced/experienced in a target culture (X)?"

3. Explain to the students the parallel practices of the target culture, making comparisons, and emphasizing similarities and differences between the students' culture and the target culture. Use visual illustrations and examples as necessary.

4. Provide succinct and relevant advice of how to behave appropriately in the target culture, if appropriate.

5. Optional: End with a short prayer related to the lesson, asking God to help us better understand each other as we work on becoming better neighbors to one another through mutual respect and cross-cultural understanding.

Geo-cultural exploration:

1. Distribute the appropriate blank maps to the students.

2. Give students historical or cultural information that they need to learn during the lesson.

3. Working in pairs, ask students to use the map provided to identify the countries and places where various people reside whom they are learning about.

4. Review the answers, making sure that everyone has the correct answers on their individual map. Show students the correct answers on the demonstration map.

5. Optional: End with a short prayer related to the lesson, asking God to help us better understand each other as we work on becoming better neighbors to one another through mutual respect and cross-cultural understanding.

Dos and don'ts for teachers:

- Do provide opportunities for students to share ideas with each other, by using the pair conversation format.

- Don't get into class debate and discussions that diverge from the topic of the lesson.

- Be on guard about your own assumptions and prejudices as you teach each Cultural Insights lesson.

- Do not over-generalize.

- Do keep the tone of the conversation respectful and bias-free.

- Don't be afraid to say "I don't know but I'll try to check with a native speaker and get back to you later".

- Do remind everyone of the basic rules.

- Do show respect for your students at all times, even when you remind them of their own prejudice.

- Don't ignore blatant prejudice and bias shared in your class discussion.

- Do pause, reflect and ask for assistance from your friends who are native speakers. They are your best guides.

Cultural Tidbits

*Culture: The customs, arts, social institutions, and achievements
of a particular nation, people, or other social group.
(New Oxford American Dictionary)*

Culture

Latino

Language

Spanish (there are also a great many indigenous languages spoken in countries across North and South America.)

The term **Latino** is an umbrella term which may be applied to persons from Latin American countries (including Brazilians who speak Portuguese). Hispanic Americans are also called Latinos, because most are of Latin-American origin. Many Hispanic people here in the U.S. identify themselves simply as Americans. There are others who identify themselves according to their cultural or national background and refer to themselves as Mexican Americans, Puerto Ricans, Cuban Americans, Chilean Americans and so on. A Chicano is a person born in the U.S. whose forebears immigrated from Mexico. Latino is the most general term of the three.

Do not refer to all Spanish speakers as "Mexican." The term **Latino** for males or **Latina** for females would be appropriate.

Names

Latinos use "doubled" last names in a particular order: first name, father's last name, mother's last name. They do not hyphenate between the two last names as we do in the United States. If there is only one last name listed, it should be the father's last name. We would properly alphabetize by father's last name, not by mother's last name. A mother may be referred to by her first name, **de** and her father's last name (e.g. Maria de Alba). Please extend the courtesy of asking a Latino student, parent or adult how they would like to be addressed.

For an extended and very clear discussion of common practice regarding names by a Puerto Rican professor at Virginia Polytechnic Institute and State University (Virginia Tech), see this blogpost at: http://perez.cs.vt.edu/twolastnames.

Time

Rigid or flexible? In mainstream American culture, time is perceived as rigid, segmented, limited and linear. Time is treated as a commodity. Time can be saved, wasted or spent wisely. "Time is money" is a well-known proverb in American culture. In contrast, many other cultures hold a different view of time. For Hispanic/Latino cultures time is flexible, elastic, relaxed, unlimited and circular.

Personal space

Touch: Latinos are affectionate, warm people who naturally hug and touch upon greeting. Embrace in greeting: Friends and people of the same social class embrace one another in greeting quite commonly. It is not uncommon that a kiss to one or both cheeks is preceded or followed by the embrace. The hug and touch varies from country to country.

Example: In Chile, upon greeting and leaving, cheek kisses are often exchanged between man and woman and between women. The kiss is more of a cheek sweep. Rather than smacking the other's cheek, both parties gently touch cheek to cheek and send the kiss to the air. The action is always performed with the right cheek, and handshakes may add to the greeting. Between men, the kissing is replaced with a hearty handshake and sometimes a pat to the shoulder.

Family/La familia

The family is a concept as well as an entity. It involves a commitment by its members to the family and extends beyond the nuclear family. The extended family, composed of grandparents, parents, children, relatives, and godparents, acts as a support system. The family frequently includes more than blood and legal relationships. Close friends can become members of the family assuming special roles and responsibilities. It is not uncommon for children and adolescents to refer to significant adults as **tío/tía** (uncle/aunt). Preschool children in particular refer to their teachers as **tío/tía.**

Holidays

- Cinco de Mayo (Spanish for "fifth of May") is a celebration held on May 5. It is celebrated in the United States and in Mexico, primarily in the state of Puebla, where the holiday is called **El Día de la Batalla de Puebla** (English: The Day of the Battle of Puebla).

- Fiestas patrias: Mexican Independence Day is widely observed by Mexicans outside and inside Mexico, on September 16. Note: The above-mentioned holidays originate in Mexico only. Persons from Central and South America have other holidays in their background. It is offensive to lump all our Spanish-speaking neighbors together as celebrants of these holidays. The U. S. celebrates Hispanic Heritage Month from September 15-October 15.

The table below (and continued on the next page) shows the dates when independence is celebrated in each of the Latin American countries:

U.S. CIA World Factbook Independence Days
Latin American Countries

Country	Independence
Argentina	9 July 1816 (from Spain)
Belize	21 September 1981 (from UK)
Bolivia	6 August 1825 (from Spain)
Brazil	7 September 1822 (from Portugal)
Chile	18 September 1810 (from Spain)
Colombia	20 July 1810 (from Spain)
Costa Rica	15 September 1821 (from Spain)
Cuba	20 May 1902 (from Spain 10 December 1898; administered by the US from 1898 to 1902)
Dominican Republic	27 February 1844 (from Haiti)
El Salvador	15 September 1821 (from Spain)
Guatemala	15 September 1821 (from Spain)
Honduras	15 September 1821 (from Spain)
Mexico	16 September 1810 (from Spain)
Nicaragua	15 September 1821 (from Spain)
Panama	3 November 1903 (from Colombia; became independent from Spain 28 November 1821)
Paraguay	14 May 1811 (from Spain)
Peru	28 July 1821 (from Spain)
Puerto Rico	none (territory of the US with commonwealth status)
Uruguay	25 August 1825 (from Brazil)
Venezuela	5 July 1811 (from Spain)

Geography

Most countries have an "official national language"; there are 14 countries in the world that have Spanish as their official language, and 6 more (and a US territory) that have Spanish as the de facto national language (marked by an * in the list below). Here is the list of countries by continent (with their capital in parenthesis):

Europe
Spain (Madrid)

Africa
Equatorial Guinea (Malabo) in West Africa

North and Central America
Mexico (Mexico City)*
Costa Rica (San José)
Cuba (Havana)
Dominican Republic (Santo Domingo)*
El Salvador (San Salvador)
Guatemala (Guatemala City)
Honduras (Tegucigalpa)
Nicaragua (Managua)*
Panamá (Panamá City)
Puerto Rico (San Juan)* [Note that Puerto Rico is not a country; it is a US Territory. Puerto Ricans are US citizens.]

South America
Argentina (Buenos Aires)*
Bolivia (La Paz)
Chile (Santiago)*
Colombia (Bogotá)
Ecuador (Quito)
Paraguay (Asunción)
Perú (Lima)
Uruguay (Montevideo)*
Venezuela (Caracas)

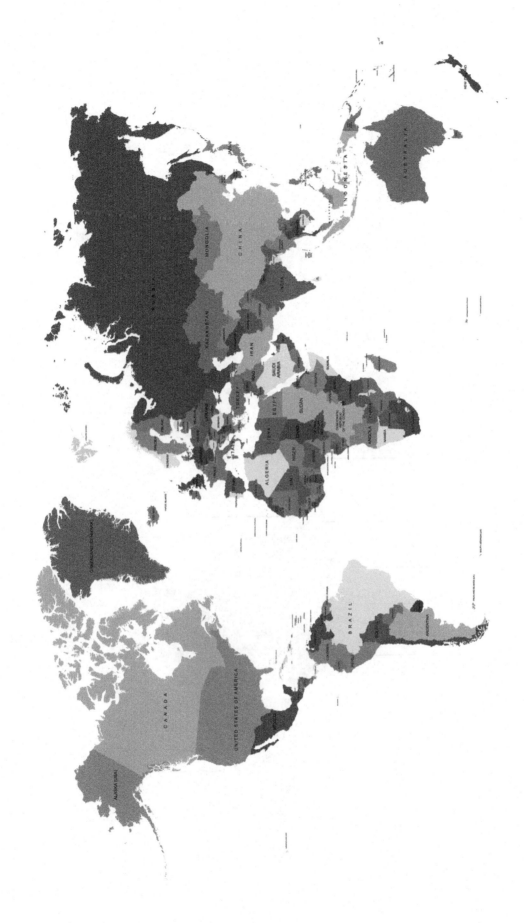

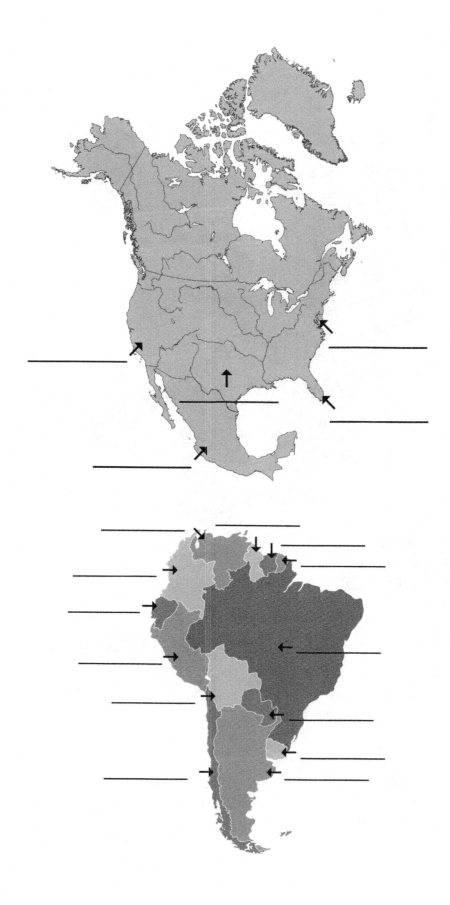

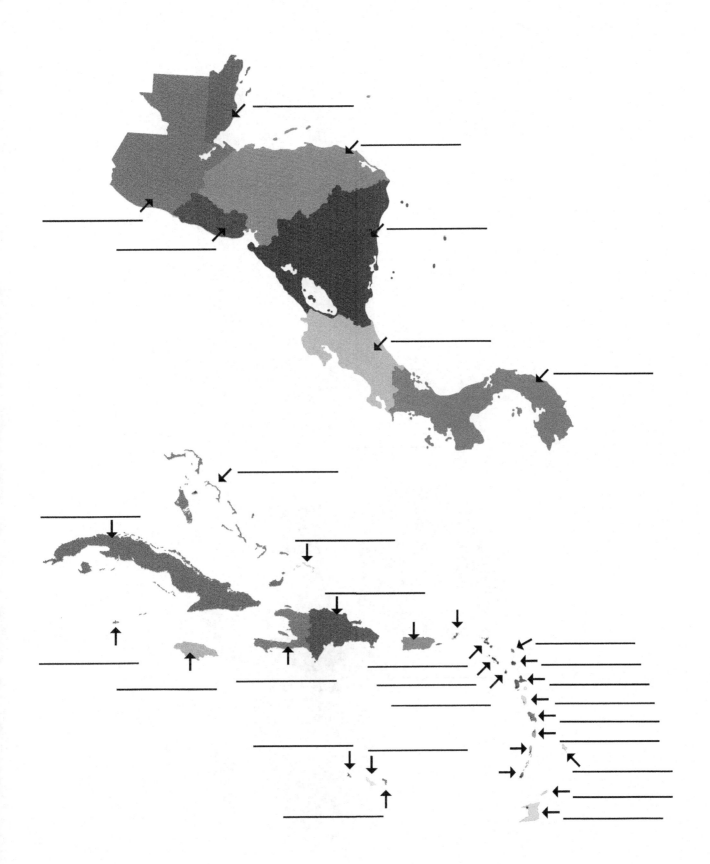

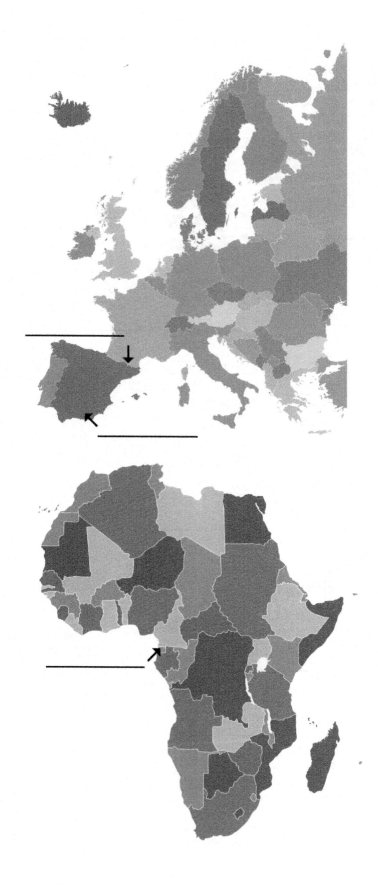

Cultural Insights: Self-Identity

Self-identity (recommended to accompany Lesson 1: La familia)

Procedure: See Geo-cultural exploration on page 57 of this manual

Materials needed:
pencil/pen
colored pencils/crayons
world map (included in Student's Manual)
blank maps (included in Student's Manual)
Cultural Tidbit on Geography (included in Student's Manual)

There are 14 countries in the world that have Spanish as their official language, and 6 more (and a US territory) that have Spanish as the de facto national language.

Ask the participants to label the maps using the Cultural Tidbit Geography on page 49 and the World Map in the Student's Manual. These documents are also to be found in this chapter of the Teacher's Manual; see pages 62-67. The objective is to have a visual of the countries and the US territory that speak Spanish as their official language, and to understand how the wide diversity of cultures among Spanish speakers comes about.

Cultural Insights: Names

Names (recommended to accompany Lesson 2: Mi vecino es...)

Procedure: See cultural comparison on page 56 of this manual

Materials needed:
whiteboard or chalkboard
chalk or dry erase marker
Cultural Tidbits on Names (included in Student's Manual)

- 2 minutes: Divide the group into pairs, and write the question on the board: How are names used in our country? Tell participants that they have two minutes to just talk.

- 10 minutes: Pull the group back together. Draw on the board two large overlapping circles. Label one circle "USA" and the other "Spanish-speaking countries". Tell them that this is called a "Venn diagram", and explain that it is just a reminder of the idea of comparison. On the board in the spaces around the diagram, briefly and quickly write the practices regarding the use of names offered by the participants that are generally acceptable in our culture. (Note: if a specific contradictory example is given, say "Thank you. This is probably an exception", but don't write it down.)

Then write--again, in the spaces around the diagram--write general information regarding common practices in Spanish-speaking cultures. Give information as opposed to asking questions for this circle. If there's something that was not talked about, simply add that information at the end.

Finally, conclude the lesson by telling them what to do if they want to know someone's name or ask how they prefer to be addressed. See the Cultural Tidbits on this topic of names. It is common to take the last name of the husband when women marry men. We have in common that we have first names and family name last. There are many practices that differ from typical US practice, and there are cross-generational differences in the US as well. Be sure to control the conversation so as to avoid long discussions of personal experience, exceptional practices, and the like. Keep the discussion general.

Cultural Insights: Personal Space and Touch

Personal space and touch (recommended to accompany Lesson 3: Me gusta, No me gusta...)

Procedure: See cultural vignette/situation on pages 56-57 of this manual

Materials needed: Refer to Cultural Tidbits (included in Student's Manual)

Situation:
You are invited to an informal get-together with some Hispanic/Latino neighbors and their family. As you enter the house, the host and the hostess come out

to greet you. Even though you extend your hand for a handshake, they instantly pull you in for a hug. You feel somewhat uncomfortable about hugging people but notice that everyone else around you are hugging each other and some even give each other a kiss on each cheek. What should you do?

Explanation:

In the Hispanic and Latino community, personal space is quite narrow. People are very affectionate and show their friendliness and hospitality with hugs and in some community, with kisses on one or both cheeks. Understanding that this gesture is an extension of hospitality will help you feel a little more at ease with this custom. Since personal space is very idiosyncratic, it will take you a while to get used to the bodily contact that accompany others' ways of greetings. If you feel more comfortable shaking hands as your greeting, do so with a friendly smile. People will understand.

Cultural Insights: The Sense of Time

The sense of time (recommended to accompany Lesson 4: El buen samaritano)

Procedure: See cultural vignette/situation on pages 56-57 of this manual

Materials needed: Refer to Cultural Tidbits (included in Student's Manual)

Situation:

You live next to a Hispanic/Latino family and have a friendly, courteous relation with your neighbors. Lately, you think that the relationship is getting a little tense since the time you invited them over for a barbecue with your family and a few other neighbors. The invitation clearly stated that the party started at 5:00PM and they had volunteered to bring appetizers. Everyone arrived on time except for the Hernandez family, who showed up an hour late, when everyone else was already for the hamburgers and hotdogs. It was an uncomfortable, awkward evening for everyone, to say the least.

• What cultural assumptions/practices may have caused the conflict in this situation?

• How would you solve the conflict if it were you?

Explanation:

Time is treated with much more flexibility in the Hispanic/Latino community. Punctuality, especially for parties, is not a customary expectation in many of the

Hispanic/Latino communities. People are typically expected to come an hour or so later than indicated in the invitation. What is important is the sense of community that is built in the gathering. People come late, hang out and often stay late to talk and have fun with each other. Being able to adjust your expectations to this cultural difference may help you not be quite bothered by your friends' and neighbors' late arrival.

Cultural Insights: Fiestas patrias

Fiestas patrias (Independence Day; recommended to accompany Lesson 5: Padre Nuestro)

Procedure:

Materials needed:
  pens/pencils
  world map (included in Student's Manual)
  blank maps (included in Student's Manual)
  Cultural Tidbits (included in Student's Manual)

Using the maps from Lesson 1, and the Cultural Tidbits for Independence Days, label each Spanish-speaking country with the date/year when it gained its independence.

Cultural Insights: Where in the World Is VIM?

Where in the world is VIM? (recommended to accompany Lesson 6: Este es mi cuerpo)

Procedure: See geo-cultural exploration on page 57 of this manual

Materials needed:
  pens/pencils
  world map (included in Student's Manual)
  blank maps (included in Student's Manual)
  Cultural Tidbit for VIM (included in Student's Manual)

Mark the countries where VIM (Volunteers In Mission) works. This lesson focuses on specific countries where the United Methodist Church has a conference and already has a lot of connection.

The Administrative Documents in the following section are materials that we found useful for planning, organizing, and running the Spanish as a Second Language program in the Northern Illinois Conference. You may adapt these documents to the needs of your own conference, district, or local church, always keeping in mind the theological foundation of this Spanish language program. Providing radical hospitality is the first and foremost goal of every aspect of the program.

FAQ: Spanish as a Second Language Classes

1. Who are these classes for?

The classes are designed for adult learners, both clergy and lay persons, who are beginners in Spanish.

2. Who is sponsoring the classes?

The Northern Illinois Conference of the United Methodist Church and its six districts (Aurora, Chicago Northwest, Chicago Southern, DeKalb, Elgin, and Rockford) are offering the classes.

3. What will I learn? How will I learn?

This class is designed to be an interactive learning experience. Many parts of the class will be conducted in Spanish, in a way that will make it easy for you to understand what's going on. You'll be exposed to at least 100 words of Spanish—enough to offer a neighborly greeting over the back fence, but not enough to carry on a fluent conversation. No one will expect you to memorize everything. You'll learn names of family members, words of welcome, telling time, a few hymns in Spanish, the story of the Good Samaritan, the Lord's Prayer, and words to tell how you feel and ask others how they are feeling. At the end of the series, you will have the opportunity to enjoy a potluck meal with Spanish speakers, and participate in the sacrament of Holy Communion in Spanish.

4. What is the goal of the classes?

The goal is to help non-Spanish speakers overcome cultural and linguistic barriers to practicing radical hospitality with our Spanish-speaking neighbors. We will learn about Hispanic cultures—the importance of family, food, fun, and caring for each other—and learn some basic Spanish, enough to feel comfortable greeting the Spanish speakers around us, ask after their children, and invite them to share God's love with our brothers and sisters in Christ. The goal is not to convert, proselytize, or badger

Spanish speakers into learning English. It is to stand on common ground with them, and open our hearts, our minds, and our doors to them.

5. How many classes are there in the series?

In general, there will be six sessions, meeting once a week for two hours. Some classes may be formatted differently for the convenience of the participants: for example, five consecutive evenings running at the same time as Vacation Bible School at the host site.

6. How large are the classes?

Each class is required to have a minimum of 12 participants, registered and prepaid, and is allowed a maximum of 20.

7. If the class I want has filled up, can I be waitlisted?

Yes! If the class you want is full, you can be waitlisted for that class. Or you can select another location. Or you can withdraw your registration and just wait for a new round of classes.

8. I already studied Spanish in high school, but I've forgotten it all. Can I take the class?

There's no pre-test. If you can't carry on a conversation in Spanish, you'll feel right at home. If you're already fluent but want the specialized content of these classes, you may prefer to wait for a more advanced class so as not to demoralize the beginners.

9. Where are the classes held?

The classes will be held at host churches around the Conference. Keep your eye on this website for announcements of future locations.

10. What if I can't attend all of the classes?

We want to make this work! Once you have registered for a class, you may attend session 1 at one location, session 2 at another, and so on. All we ask is that you notify the teacher at the "guest" site you would like to attend, to make sure that there is room for you at that class meeting.

11. How much do the classes cost?

The cost of each class is a flat fee of $400 for up to 12 participants. Additional participants, up to a total of 20 for the class, may enroll at $30 each. The minimum number of 12 participants may be reached from within the local congregation, by sharing numbers and costs with a neighboring church, or by inviting community members to participate. If a Host Church is unable to enroll at least 12 participants through any of these paths, they may pay the full $400 fee and run the class with a smaller number. Please note that all fees must be prepaid before the class can be authorized and a teacher can be supplied.

The class expenses, including your teacher's honorarium and travel expenses and the cost of producing the classroom materials, are partially covered by this fee. If you wish to donate further to help cover the costs of the Spanish as a Second Language program, you can send a check to:

Rev. Michael Mann, Northern Illinois Conference, Program Office, 217 Division Street, Elgin, IL 60120

or give your donation to your church office. All donations should be marked "Spanish." Please see #16 below for more information.

12. How do I register?

Look for the Student Registration Form on this page. Fill it out and email it to ssl@umcnic.org, or mail it to Northern Illinois Conference, Program Office, 217 Division St., Elgin, IL 60120. You'll find a list of currently available classes here too, with contact information for each site.

13. Why are you doing this?

Spanish as a Second Language seeks to act upon the continuing Conference mission statement: Who is my neighbor? More importantly, it seeks to translate this seminal question into concrete action in our communities. It acknowledges the fact that in many cases Hispanic and Anglo communities do not mix, and that because of this we fail to fully serve God and love our neighbor.

The project seeks to break down the language and cultural barriers among us so that we can know our neighbors and understand their ways. We propose to accomplish this by giving our Anglo congregants the opportunity to learn the language of their neighbor, to enable them to speak—if only a little—with Hispanic neighbors. In so doing, the participants will themselves be transformed, and we will thus transform our relationships with those around us.

By focusing Spanish classes on ways in which we serve and love our neighbor, rather than on the usual grammatical or secular-activity approaches such as travel, we will open the doors for worshipping together (participants will be invited to worship in a Hispanic church) as well as eating together (the last class of the series includes a potluck), sharing each other's burdens, praying with and for each other, and truly becoming one in the Lord. We will be recreating the miracle of Pentecost.

14. Can I sign up my whole family?

The classes are designed for adult learners aged 18 and above. There are many opportunities in most communities for children to learn Spanish, and the presence of children in the class calls for adherence to Safe Sanctuaries rules. Besides, sharing what you have learned in the class with your children makes a great family activity. Any requested exception must be directed to the SSL Team via Rev. Michael Mann.

15. Is babysitting available?

That's up to each host church. If they have the facilities and can provide the service in accordance with Safe Sanctuaries principles, they may make babysitting available. Participants are responsible for inquiring about childcare and notifying the SSL Local Church Ambassador each week if childcare will be needed.

16. I'd like to make a donation to help support the classes. How do I do that?

Thank you! We appreciate the support! You can write a check made out to "Northern Illinois Conference", and send it to Rev. Michael Mann, Northern Illinois Conference, Program Office, 217 Division Street, Elgin, IL 60120. You can call him at (847) 931-0710x20 and make a donation by credit card. Or you can send your donation to one of the host churches. In all cases, please be sure to mark your donation clearly with "SSL" or "Spanish".

17. I am a Spanish teacher. I'd like to help by teaching a class. What should I do?

Look for the job description and job application on this page (www.umcnic.org/ssl). Please note that this is a ministry. Our teachers are volunteers who are offered an honorarium and a travel allowance (round-trip from teacher's residence to host location, using your odometer reading for each week, recorded on the NIC Reimbursement Form).

18. I'm signed up for a class! Do I have to buy a book?

All the materials you need will be provided! You will receive a packet of handouts that will give you a record of the information presented, and offer ways for you to practice at home.

19. Can I get on an email list to get more information when it's available?

Sure! Look for the link on this page (www.umcnic.org/ssl). We will not share your email address with anyone else, and will use it only for the purpose of sharing information about the Spanish as a Second Language classes.

20. Are the classes open to community members?

Yes, they are! First choice will be given to members of the host church, then to other members in the Conference, and then to the community as a whole.

21. Do I have to be a United Methodist to join a class?

No, you don't! If there's room in the class and you share the goals of the class, you are welcome.

22. Will there be advanced classes at some point?

Yes, Level 2 is now in preparation!

23. When will there be a class closer to me?

Keep checking back on this page to see a list of all currently available classes, and also future classes that have been announced. Please let us know if there is a location where you would like to see a class offered!

CPSIA information can be obtained at www.ICGtesting.com
Printed in the USA
LVOW03s0638310715

448359LV00004B/15/P